Paradise

Also by Victoria Redel

Poetry

Already the World

Swoon

Woman Without Umbrella

Fiction

Where the Road Bottoms Out

Loverboy

The Border of Truth

Make Me Do Things

Before Everything

Paradise

Victoria Redel

Four Way Books
Tribeca

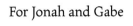

For Jonah and Gabe

Library of Congress Cataloging-in-Publication Data

Names: Redel, Victoria, author.
Title: Paradise / Victoria Redel.
Description: [New York] : Four Way Books, [2022] | Identifiers: LCCN 2021046733
ISBN 9781954245136 (trade paperback)
ISBN 9781954245211 (epub)
Subjects: LCGFT: Poetry.
Classification: LCC PS3568.E3443 P37 2022 | DDC 811/.54--dc23
LC record available at https://lccn.loc.gov/2021046733

This book is manufactured in the United States of America and printed on
acid-free paper.

Four Way Books is a not-for-profit literary press. We are grateful for the assistance
we receive from individual donors, public arts agencies, and private foundations
including the NEA, NEA Cares, Literary Arts Emergency Fund, and the
New York State Council on the Arts, a state agency.

We are a proud member of the Community of Literary Magazines and Presses.

Contents

1

2

Where is the main stress, for instance, in *being-there* (entre-là): on *being* or on *there*? In *there*—which it would be better to call *here*—shall I first look for my being?

—Gaston Bachelard

So you're here? Straight from a moment still ajar?

—Wisława Szymborska

1

The Border

There was a gate & through the gate
another garden—

same grasses, clover, gentian violet & lily
& the dry winds also made those willows sway—

just that rusty gate—
the dirt beneath scraped when it hinged open then shut—

& some claimed one side was Paradise.

Garden

In the first weeks, we already knew
this was history,

that you'd speak of our nakedness,
the flat grasses we wove & slipped over

each other. First there were frills of green
leaf, stalks, tips too. Later came wild

onion, the sharp tang of shoot & bulb.
Then peaches. Standing together in sunlight,

of course, praise & song. We hardly cared
that you would get so much of it wrong,

that you would always speak of an apple or claim
that one of us was so persuaded by the snake.

Darlings, we imagined *you*. Over & over, how
you would break each other. Wound this garden.

Only then, still licking the dried peach juice
sticky down our fingers, did we know shame.

Dominion

The animals had no love for us.
We did not lie tenderly with the lion.

& we had no peaceable gathering
with the alligator & the wasp.

Nor for a moment did the crow
believe we had dominion.

& if you had heard that caw
& had seen clouds massing

from steady hooves,
you would understand

there was never a fall.
We stood; we ran.

Sixth Day

Already "butterfly" & "panther," "frog" & "muskrat,"
already the "horse's tail" switching "flies." For days
flock wing of "sparrow" & "flamingo," "gnat"
& "cricket" swarm. Already pounding herd of "cattle,"
"elephant," "zebra." Already "jellyfish" immortal
& "hatchetfish" spinning its own cold light.
Each day "termites" mounding their saliva & shit.
& yes, already "trees" each with distinct "fruit,"
"seed," "leaf rot," "root" & dialects of "soil."
So, on the day we showed up, not one creature waited
to be named. There was no amazement at our upright
posture, our furless skin. Instead, they humbly sent forth
the tiny "mosquito." Then the "tsetse," the "louse"
& "bot fly" joined in to clarify the situation.

Temptation

Another thing:
we always knew we would leave.

Some days it was all too rampant,
the ground pulpy with fallen fruit—

so we invented hunger.

Bored, we turned away
from each heavy luscious bough.

We'd dreamed of a door—
one cheek pressed to the painted wood.

This was our only appetite.

Just to be alone
even for a few breaths,

on that other side
after the knock.

Origin

But doesn't every story begin with expulsion?

Gate.   River.   Wind & the difficult
woods.   Hair cropped.   A changed name.

An uncovered head.   Refusal to kneel.   Lilac polish
on a son's toes.   A daughter on a tire swing,
  her cotton skirt lifting.

& where is your forest?   Your shame?
       How far will it send you?

Also, of course, unexpected love.

Betrayals commence.   A gentle neighbor turns you in
  for a sack of flour.   A child sold

then sold again.

By now you understand not everyone gets to live through this.

      But *you're* alive—
& who remains to assess your choice or bribe?

Still, that sticky shame.

You Called It Paradise

The gate had a broken latch,
a thin curved deer rib
fastened it shut.

Every day we walked out
to the mossy edge. We were restless.
It is not true that we fled

at the end, or that it was an end.
When we found the gate,
of course, we opened it.

Exodus

We came from somewhere.   Had a village, & then didn't.

*

Trees broke in wind. A river went dry. Men arrived. A gang. A mob.
More by night. Fires were set. Then rains pressed through a neighbor's
door. We salvaged. Spoon & shoe. But might have chosen better. We
knew the importance of bedding.

*

It's simple math:

The want   &   the want   &   the want.

*

Don't talk about one long list of sorry.

*

Let's go, we say standing still.

*

In my grandmother's trunk I found a boat. In my grandmother's trunk
I found a boat & a train. In my grandmother's trunk I found a boat,
a train, August wind, the river Prut, an uncle in prison, a book of
addresses, a box of faces.

*

Identity papers were stamped.   At some point:

                    our name twisted to local consonants.

*

Look at the box of faces.   Worry & dignity.   What to do with the careful
dress, the good suit, the unpeeled orange in an open hand?   In smudged
pencil, on the back of each face, names I don't recognize.   No one left to ask.

Refugees

In the last days, when he could barely open his eyes,
he'd look up from the hospital bed, lift his hand & say, That's me.

& we said, Yes, Poppa. You're right here.

No, he said, jabbing his finger towards the television—clusters
    of makeshift tents
bent under gusting winds, a child held over the rail of a listing boat.

Or he pointed at lines of young men, squatting men, men
slouched against stone walls, sweatshirts tied around waists,
    a few smoking cigarettes.

No, he said, waving toward men, browner & blacker than he;
You think that's not me, he said. You, look again.

We Petition You, Sirs,

On behalf of our brother who resided ... It has come to our attention that what was once our home ... There was a forest ... There was a house ... Behind the forest, a clearing, where our mother ... On behalf of branches ... On behalf of iron veined through the hillside ... Our brother who was rescinded ... The creek ran heavy in ... Our brother removed ... The keys were under the ... Whereby the heirs of those ... Below please find directions ... Where our brother was once ... The exact address is ... That said, our brother's whereabouts are unknown ... Half the family was ... Kindly look under the floor ... The address, no longer available due to ... Where the rock cleaves ... The entrance to our ... The dry creek, by the razed forest, when the ... The watch repair shop where our father ... We understand new occupants are residing ... On behalf of moss ... The third stair up ... According to Ordinance ... Where the board creaks ... To all appearances he was deported & killed by ... According to damaged water ... The papers were ... Whereby the heirs of those who have suffered damages caused ... That said, my brother owned a house ... Under Title 11 of the War Claims Act ... The undersigned ... Of stateless nationality, born in ... At present temporarily residing in ... As war refugee, as climate refugee, as political refugee ... Hereby declare ...

The Other Child

Have you also always waited for disaster?
They tuck you in. *Sleep, child*. But you're

not asleep. Last train, last boat & don't look
back where another child now sleeps in your bed,

wears your green wool coat to school. You never lived
in the shattered city. Never crossed their river.

Still each day at school the house is on fire.
The parents tremble like overtired children.

Do you smell the burning wool?

Humankind Sonnets, *a Grammar*

1. Subject/Verb

We roamed. We razed. We abducted. We burned.
We infected. We birthed. We raised. We stormed.

We deforested, cradled, salvaged, praised.
We locked up, locked down, locked out, in. We slaved.

We sewed. We sang. We enslaved. We broke.
We cracked, peeled, grabbed, bled. We denied. We choked.

We held, healed, built. We roughed, split. We felled.
We slit. We severed, gashed, stormed, shot. We shelled.

We bowed, bowed to. We ripped off, ripped out.
We broke down, broke in. We cut up, cut out.

We tended. We kissed. We starved, fattened, raped.
We hung up, hung out. We shot, shattered, raped.

We raped. We raped. We raped. We raped. We gassed.
Sold. Bought. Kneeled. Reaped. Degraded. Amassed.

2. Object

grandmothers, neighbors, genitals, infants,
monks, teeth, feet, teachers, sisters, elephants,
houses, families, eyes, skulls, temples, aunts,
villages, whales, doctors, brothers, migrant
workers, wolves, bears, skin, oceans, bees, pregnant
women, tigers, necks, fingers, bones, merchants,
babies, uncles, nuns, turtles, street urchins,
forests, hospitals, churches, servants,
fathers, mothers, newborns, yurts, tenements,
tongues, huts, tents, housing developments,
frogs, redwoods, dirt, snowy owls, pelicans,
air, water, ozone, glaciers, dirt, sediment,
cells, molecules, atoms, stars, elements,
her, him, you, me, they, breath & sentient.

3. Preposition

In summer, in truth, in safety, in rain,
Under veil, blanket, obligation, sway,
Against stone, against storm, drift, against strain,
Despite wood, below wool, from night, since gray,

Without warning, without water, light, play,
Without access, without breasts, without fear,
Near miss, near to the heart, near disarray,
For the sake of, for the taking, for being queer,

Next to the bridge, the bed, from mouth, from ear,
Since forever, since never, since the flood,
Through the onslaught, the bounty, through that year,
With kindness, words, with river clay, with blood,

From you, from me, between us, between them,
Out of reckless broke, mend then breaks, then mend

Babel

Then we stepped together off the curb
into the Empire's cracked streets

& what I could see of his left side below
the green plaid shorts—
thigh, calf & the delicate turn of ankle
&, also, from his T-shirt—
whole arm, hand, neck—was spotted
gold & black,
in lavishly rendered cheetah,

then, at the corner crossing, side-by-side—
his face—half-patterned & whiskered.
Eventually I'll do all of it, he said,
his unpigmented fingers flourishing
a figure in the air.
But does it hurt? I asked.
Which side would you be asking about? he said.

Years ago, when I first arrived to that city,
I walked behind a stranger.

Speaking of Men

Then began the exemptions.

My sons. Your brothers. Grandfathers who left
with nothing.   A neighbor boy who put hands
to where hands had been put on him.   The drugged
boy. Beaten boy. Hunted boy. Lost boy. Starved
boy. Forgotten boy. Skittish boy. Boy of
a mother who had three jobs. Soft boy. Strapped
down boy. Transit boy. Boy who watched what should
never be watched. Boy given the gun. Boy
who can't sleep remembering what was done
& what he did when the burnt sky fell & he saw

the other broken boys scatter & begin to run.

Tributary

Is it just me or does every immigrant's child have memories
of a marshy bank overflowing & someone gutting fish?

If I'm walking the path hugging the Hudson,
how is it I'm in Romania, birthing my mother in a high bed,

in another home the family abandons just in time?
Come on, I'm nobody's child anymore.

Everything is just in time. Another war
in another disputed city, wrapped in a frayed kilim,

my days crowded & official, five years of bribe
the guard takes while Matus wastes in solitary.

Nights in the Ural Mountains displaced person's camp,
Aunt Reva's frozen, toeless feet burn against my legs.

Now a lush spring, floods of refugees camp along the Seine
& Persian papers keep a star off my mother's coat.

Then memory's torrent, the boat tipped, suitcases
lost, lines of history snapped. I'm wrist sunk,

searching the tributary of the Prut & Danube.
A tugboat nudges a freighter up the ice-chunked Hudson.

My vigilance recovers nothing more than the tang
of silt & pike. It costs, even still, to cross to the other side.

If You Knew

He wanted to take the muddy stream where he sang with frogs.
She wanted to take dawn in the linden tree.
They left a reed basket of wind.
He wanted the resin of August.
She left the feather grass of an evening walk.
They left all the tender minutes unbuttoning her blouse.
She wanted to pack the folded sun from the linen closet.
He wanted to take the shuffle of her slippers on the stairs.
She wanted her mother's fingers rummaging through the button box.
He wanted the Steppe's black soil.
They left moss between stones, the steel winter light in the room
    where she sewed, the jiggle of a key in the front door.
They left a cupboard of embroidered afternoons.

*

What would you take?
If you had a month, a week, an evening, an hour?
If there were no one looking, no one saying: Don't take that! Why take that?
What would you take if you thought it was temporary
relocation, transient, provisional, short-term shelter?
If you couldn't use your ATM card, your credit card, cash in your stock,
sell your home, get a supervisor on the phone, charge your phone.
If you couldn't keep your phone?

What would you take if you knew you'd never come back?
What would you take if you lost track of the children?

Assimilation

Our children didn't want our stories of the animals.
No torrents of frog, swarms, & the lamb,
they claimed, tangled their dreams with mange.

If we tried to speak of the lost people
they covered their soft ears
against dust & burnt ribs of desert wind.

No, to stories of the sea. No, to the forest.
Even our small garden was forbidden. Don't make us
imagine, pleaded our children, if you did or didn't hide.

We, who stole the trout's fin to cross a river,
who typed the fox's & the snake's names on our passports,
stayed mostly quiet.

So much will not be said.

How could they hold our hands if they knew
what we'd done with our hands?
Or that before them, once upon a time, other children.

Lucky Dog

& today, more than fifty years later,
I'm wondering did they name him Lucky—the dog

that showed up on our front step—because our parents
saw him as a reminder of their own luck

that they actually lived in a house with front steps,
when between them they could count on one hand

the childhood friends that were not dead? No, let me
be clear. Was the difficult & loyal German shepherd,

Lucky, who roamed the tidy neighborhood
then nightly returned to our meat scraps & mat,

their penitence, our parents leaning out
the kitchen door calling & calling & calling him back.

Last Picnic, Galați

At the end of what my mother calls the last Sunday
in the Galați garden: wine in cups, candles, plates of almond cake,
& cherry pits staining the embroidered tablecloth,
her father announced that leaving, she'd choose one dog.

Like you, cherie, my mother says, I was a girl of eight &
I cried, insisted I wouldn't leave without Bijou & Beau.
Then her father lifted her onto his lap & one by one,
pressed my mother's small fingers into warm beeswax.

This little survivor, he sang to the thumb. This brave survivor,
to the pointer, like the song about going off to market.
But my pinkie, my mother says, he turned this way & that,
kissed twice, put it close to the candle but never pressed in.

Then her father peeled the wax scallops off the other fingers,
admiring the etch of each print before melting over flame.
Two days later, my mother says, we fled, Bijou tucked in my coat.
But what about Beau? I say, hugging her. What happened to Beau?

You don't see? she says, her voice turned flinty, pushing me off.
She points to my dolls, my books, my bed, my closet of dresses,
the ceiling, the floor, out the window to our car on the street.
This isn't about some little dog, my mother says, this is about your life.

A True Story

Chapter 1

Let me tell you a true story I was told.

My great grandfather played flute in the orchestra of the Turkish Sultan.

He was a composer in the Sultan's orchestra.

Chapter 2

This is what I've been told.

Chapter 3

But is this all I know?

Chapter 4

Here's a little more.

My great grandfather was nicknamed The Little Sultan

by the Turkish Sultan himself &, at some point, then, or later,

the name became Russianized as Soltanitzky.

Chapter 5

Is this actually what happened?

Chapter 6

So many parts of this story I'll never know.

Chapter 7

I don't know if my great grandfather was born in Turkey or Russia or Egypt, but I know he died in Constantinople while my grandfather was a boy in Egypt. Why was my great grandfather not in Alexandria with his family? Why was his family not with him in Constantinople? I do know my grandfather was eleven when his father died & that he provided for his mother & sister. What could a boy sell on the streets of Alexandria? I don't know when he took his mother & sister to Russia, but I do know that in 1918 his mother & sister were dead, that my young grandfather fled Russia for Romania, that in 1938, a husband & a father, he fled Romania for Paris with Persian passports & in 1942 he fled Paris for Lisbon securing passage for his family on a boat to New York City.

Chapter 8

During the 1979 oil embargo my mother called my college dorm, her voice a panicked whisper, *Don't tell anyone my passport was Persian.*

Chapter 9

I am the first generation in my family whose children were born in the same country as their parents.

Chapter 10

How my mother had a Persian passport is not altogether another story.

Chapter 11

Why does any of this old story matter? Read the newspaper. Please, read it now. Do you have a map of the world? The map keeps changing. About those who could not cross the borders, I have spared you their true stories.

Occupation

My mother bled when the Germans entered Paris.
She was nine. The red rust ran
a wet track in her underpants like a skid mark
from the soldier's motorcycle stationed at the corner of Rue de Messine.
How could she tell her parents?
She was in love with the handsome soldier
who squatted next to her to scratch Bijou's puppy ear.
You're a fine young lady, he said impressed with her German.
She'd been hit right then, kicked in the belly
by the dimpled smile he smiled at her.
Better than the smiles of all of her first loves,
Buster Crabb, Cary & Gary & Henri Garat.
Wasn't this the truer cinema? He'd been commanded
to kill her—but their love!—he couldn't, can't
fire & only wounds her,
a bloody hurt no one else can see. She'd never tell.
My mother washes out her cotton underpants,
hides them in the armoire to dry, lies flat on the bed to quiet the blood.
In the shuttered living room, her parents argue again.
They could still get to Bordeaux. Maybe they'd been wrong
turning back on the crowded road? Isn't the Occupation safer;
with Persian papers they won't be forced to register.
But my mother knows her soldier must know the truth.
It's part of their beautiful tragedy, to hold her bloody & bandaged

in his arms as she confesses, I'm a Jew.

Natalie, darling, he'll say, I'll always protect you,

& nibble Bijou's ears. His smile! He'll carry her home.

He'll show her parents there's no reason to hide.

Getting Close

Because my mother loved pocketbooks,
I come alive at the opening click or close of a metal clasp.

& sometimes, unexpectedly, a faux crocodile handle makes me weep.

Breathy clearing of throat, a smooth arm, heels on pavement,
she lingers, sound tattoos.

I go to the thrift store to feel for bobby pins caught in the pocket seam
of a camel hair coat.

I hinge a satin handbag in the crease of my arm. I buy a little
change purse with its curled & fitted snap.

My mother bought this for me. This was my mother's.

I buy & then I buy & then, another day, I buy something else.

In Paris she had a dog, Bijou, & when they fled Paris, 1942, they left the dog.

When my mother died on February 9, 1983, she left me.

Thirty years later, I am exactly her age.

I tell my husband I will probably die by the end of today. All day he says,
Are you getting close, Sweetheart? & late in the afternoon, he asks if he
should buy enough filet of sole for two.

From a blue velvet clutch I take out a mirror & behold my lips in the
small rectangle.

Put on something nice, my mother whispers on the glass.
Let him splurge & take you out for dinner.

Another Long Story

Why don't you ever
call out
the names
of your lost,
during Remembrance Service?
the boy asks.
If I began,
his grandfather says
touching the boy's head,
we'd be here
all night,
& we want
to eat dinner.

Expulsion

Down to help out with the cooking, the shopping, driving to the dialysis clinic, paying the unpaid bills, managing the ever-growing array of unmanaged situations; so morning & evenings I also took out my father's dog, Teddy, an apricot poodle who, at the first sight of another dog, any dog, every damn walk, let's say for this evening's purpose, the bull mastiff walked by a small, bent over gentleman who was once, like my father, clearly a taller man, the spine in its seemingly inevitable compression, my father's poodle, at the sight of this bull mastiff, barked, yapped, leapt, bit at the air, bit at his leash but I kept walking, so the dog, with its snapping & twisting antics, was half-dragged, half-aloft & the gentleman asked with his elegant Spanish, maybe Venezuelan, maybe Cuban or Salvadoran accent, *How's he doing?* by which, it was clear, he meant my father, not the poodle. I said, *Fine, thank you,* yanking the dog, now airborne like a cartoon version of a frustrated, furious dog. & the gentleman said, *Your father & me, all us refugees, same story,* while he bent his already bent-over body slowly, slowly to the ground to scoop up his mastiff's monumental shit & then, even slower, with the dog waiting patiently beside him, the gentleman managed, actually leaning on his dog for balance, to gather himself upright, &, holding the bag, he turned, dropped it in the mesh wastebasket & said—*Not for babies, this business.*

Alexandria

You must go to our city, says the Egyptian coffee shop owner
at the corner of Centre and Grand
when I say my grandfather was also born in Alexandria.

Please, you must go soon, he says mornings
I come in for take-out coffee, egg & hot sauce—
no cheese, no bacon—on whole wheat,

though some days, as if resigned that I'm still here,
he just palms my change on the counter.
What is *my city? My country?* Is homeland

the Egypt of one? Warsaw, the other?
Brussels, Paris, Toulouse, Reni, Galați,
Constantinople, Lisbon, Perpignan. Every city,

a boat to a next refuge. But this morning,
along with a classic NYC diner coffee & toast,
he says, You have the true eyes of our Alexandria,

& all day, wherever I go, the thick of my almond eyes
with the dark crescent shadows I've hated since childhood,
are beautiful, an indelible mark on the atlas of my diaspora.

They Had No Choice

She thought it was more than clear,
obvious, a non-discussion given recent events,

so she was surprised, a bit
disappointed if she were honest,

that it actually involved convincing & that later,
years after they'd lived in that New World,

he continued to speak in such a manner that made her understand
he believed they would one day return.

Ordinary Sight

It isn't *beshert* that he's practically my relative, Baruch de Spinoza,
whose name means blessing, or that in Amsterdam, 1656,

he went from Synagogue's devout darling,
to convicted by the Herem for *abominable heresies*

which he practiced and taught, &, with a single horn's echo
through the temple's inky darkness, Baruch, just 23,

cursed he by day and cursed he by night, was excommunicated,
tossed, forbidden pardon, conversation or home—

but that by trade he was a lens cutter, an Oculist.
Oculist! What joy to say out loud!

Isn't it apt proof of his singular substance—
the visionary mind in a poorly lit optometrist's workshop,

grinding glass angled to the lathe, a mind enlightened
by the refractive bend of glass? He cut the distance lens

identifying Saturn's rings then another to study
vessels in the intestines' folds. *In reality,* he wrote,

is the light of the mind. He never looked for transit
to a next world. Here, he polished ordinary sight.

If you want the present to be different than the past,
he wrote, *study the past.* & then, overcome

by dust inhalation, dust of glass & diamond,
Baruch Benidito de Spinoza was dead at 44.

This morning, light curves along my teacup,
fringes the double tulips—shipped from Holland,

I wish I could tell him, 365 years later
we've dilated, recut our lens transparent & free

of superstitions; body & mind wholly integrated,
no one imprisoned, cast out, murdered for an idea.

Whatever is, is in God, all honored, not human
likeness any more than fern, atom, song, or shift of wind.

*I do not know how to teach philosophy without becoming
a disturber of the peace.* Most days I wish a world

more disturbed by Baruch's geometrics, incited
by love & clarity; a diamond's cuts, radical, incisions,

not to harm but hold, whole, a just world.

Exile Fragment

Mother, the east   her hooded eyes

The scent of our front yard lilac   her blossom that brief

Siege

After the big snow, Nana parts the red curtains & hurries us
outside with shovels to clear the deckled path of memory.

Then smoked eggplant, red pepper & salmon wrapped in spiced dough.

When the Tsar's winter carriage rumbles through the village,
our shovels strike through ice to the slate path.

Bombs away, we shout like good Cossacks—ready to charge our front door.

Last Days

It took both daughters to lift our father
from the mechanical bed
then down into the straight-backed chair
where he sat naked,
close to a fan; wet towels
patch-worked over the raw welts,
oxygen pronged up his nose,
Foley catheter bag strapped to his leg—
clawing & raking at his skin despite the gloves.

Once, when he could barely talk or lift his head,
he tugged it up a little, tilted it.
Do you need something? we said,
& he raised just an eyebrow
that way he signaled, Watch out,
when we were girls & got a little too mouthy.
What do you need? we said again
& that eyebrow perked higher,
delighted to still be the boss.

Unto

It was not the first or last time I'd lied to him.

Yesterday, belted in a row with strangers, I watched the flight tracker
   to see how easily I move across the world.

At baggage claim, luggage circled anonymously.

A boy shouted, I can do that!—pointing to a poster, a cowboy's
   arm aloft, the other rope-tied to the bull
for what rodeo calls the most dangerous eight seconds.

Of course, you can, his mother said grabbing two duffels.

This will help, I told my father with each drop of morphine.
   Let go, I said. It'll all be ok.

& it was. But only for a little while.

The Immigrant's Last Task

—as during all the years he held steady
while his American daughters crossed
a street, fell off a bike, left a party, got out
of the wrong boy's car, broke a nose, split
a lip, drove cliff roads, got a transfusion,
another surgery, lost a baby, a job,
a marriage, our mother

—he held on while my sister dodged lights,
swerved through traffic, parked, ran, & pushed
till she was next to me by his bedside,
& then, knowing his children were safe,
our father stopped steadying to let go.

2

The Psychic

He said I must pay special attention in cars. He wasn't, he assured me,
saying that I'd be in an accident but that for two weeks some particular
caution was in order, &, he said, all I really needed to do was throw
the white light of Alma around any car I entered & then I'd be fine. &
when I asked about Alma, he said, Oh, come on, you know Alma well.
You two were together first in Egypt & then at Stonehenge, & I nodded
though I've never been—in this life at least—to Stonehenge; then I
said, Shouldn't I always throw the white light of Alma around a car? &
when he said, Well, it wouldn't hurt, I said, What about around planes,
houses? What if I throw the white light of Alma around anyone who
might need protection from the reckless speed of driving or the reckless
swerve & skid of the world? & the psychic opened his hands & shrugged
up his shoulders. So despite your doubt or mine as to why I'd gone there,
to a psychic, in—I kid you not—a town of psychics—in the first place,
right now, as you read this, let me throw the white light of Alma around
you & everyone you pass close to today, beloved or stranger, the grocer,
the bus driver, the boy on his longboard, the lady you stand silent beside
in the elevator, & also I am throwing it around anyone they care about
anywhere in the spin of the world, because, we can agree that these days,
everywhere, particular caution is in order &, even if unverifiable, the
light of my dear sister Alma, couldn't hurt.

Snake

After at most a year, maybe two,
showing off how it circled their necks,
slid down & out the bottom
of a T-shirt, how they fed mice-on-ice
from an open palm, jaw unhinging
to take it whole, my sons had no time
for the snake when she'd go milky-eyed,
slowing until her dry length coiled
into days & days of such gray stillness
I'd knock the glass tank to make sure
she was alive. Then, maybe I'd be
making the bunk bed or folding
baseball pants when the edging began,
a restless roughing against bark chips,
rubbing forward along every
available friction until the split
when she'd press out of herself, leaving
the long opaque shed. I loved it
every time. I don't mean the emergence—
though, yes, there was that, how she'd fold
& stretch, glossy & clear-eyed—No,
I loved the papery, scaled ghost
I'd lift up, not to commemorate
her chance to begin again, but
the cold indifference to whom she'd been.

Bearded Iris

I have wintered hard.
Ice-sheathed, worried & weighted, a broken stalk.

Still, I walk through a darkened city of old argument,
the dense grid of streets, crumbling stoops

& someone at every corner shouting, *Cut it out.*

Then, this morning, your split parchment &
undressed blue petals.

That brave shivering & brief opening.

Brace

Those years & years—child
   bones unfixed—braced
pelvis to chin—I was encased—
   all day, all night,
a freak—a girl without a body;
    mechanical & metal barred—
I was embedded, strapped
   upright—the spine sibilant, slipped
& girdled
   against genetic mishap.

If the girl I was
   was a twisted sideshow,
day by year, I conjured
   fantastic survivals, leap
       & flame,
unroped & arial,
   a glorious *what happened to you* of lies.

One day—a woman by now
   —I am unshelled—
ta dah!—
   unbent, corrected—set
straight among the Able,

no gawkers anymore double-taking
my catastrophe.

Only now do I begin
    to understand
the shellack of their apparent normal,
    that exhausting required symmetry,
their fixed
    determination to cloak the tic,
coif the frazzle.
    It hurts to watch.

Here I stand
    on the corner of Invisible
& No One,
    sent from the tribe of the jagged,
the limper, the broken,
    pieced & caulked.
I sing for all flagrant bodies. Holy
    psalm of vitiligo, of stutter & club foot.
Freedom hymn of palsy & syndrome.
    Aria of the outward adjusted.
All awry, we are all
    what happens.
Each exceptional exception.

On the Matter of Creation

& the art teacher handed
out blobs of clay &, with
the flat of your fingers, you rolled
out the worm, roping it longer,
then coiling around & around
to build up your little cup or pot &
maybe the coil split & broke, maybe
the pot was lopsided, so wonky you
smashed it with a fist, rounding
the clay to a new smooth ball
you poked your thumb into, right
down into the center, squeezing
water from the sponge, thinning
walls you pinched from inside
& out—& you squished
this one too when a pot across
the table looked better; & when the kid
who always broke rules shaped
a thing so beautiful & weird
she didn't get in trouble this time,
you kept at it, kept shaping,
remaking the same gray clump,
until you finally thought,
this one's really good or, *it's good enough,*

& carved your initials into the soft,
flat bottom, hurrying to clean
your tools so there was a little free time
to mess around in the hallway
before the big biology test—
all this to say: this is not a parable
nor will it be when a voice declares
what is worthy, what counts
&, henceforth, which
subjects matter.

Stuck Human

Still I envy the girls who were horses,

who nickered & whinnied through school

hallways, came to the lunch table for hay,

bucked, bolted with their herd, & ran hard.

Other girls claimed an animal. Cats with milk

throated purrs circled clusters of spider girls,

leggy & fatal in black tights & boots.

But I am just as I was then, stuck human,

opposable, & reluctant, two arch fallen feet,

my only possible transformation this language,

our infinite, recursive tongue.

Mount Lafayette Elegy, 1982

Not New Hampshire on that clear day. Not
the summit ridge. Not the sudden cold drop,
the squall, the dark, fast cloud. But just one
lightning crack. For three hours, her husband pushed
& pushed & pushed her chest. Not that she was 24.

I called her Goat, a childish nickname. She pressed
her palms against my skull, claimed to make the world small.
Whatever we postured, we were still mostly child,
younger than my youngest son.

Yes, sons. That's part of how a story shifts.

Sometimes it takes so long to tell a story.
& when you do it's altered in the telling.

It isn't mine to tell her husband's story.
Or her father's drive through the night
before her mother would hear the morning broadcast.
I was her friend. Not the only one.

That summer I slept in a tent at the edge
of a field & woke each day raw & feral.

By that February my mother was dead. By stroke,
by tumor, by lung, by car, by vein, by starvation,
by miscarriage, by heart, by pill, by mind,
in the flower of alpine meadows, in the hour
of derelict streets, in the aftermath of ICUs,
my grief has never had to scavenge far.

I have waited in fields for lightning
that also would take me. & sometimes the world
was too small. I have met other beasts.
They stalk. They curl close. A purr, a thrum.
You have yours. & you. & you. & you.
I could not save my sons
their grief, could not choose
what creature travels beside them,
nor recognize its shape.

Goat, I'm old enough to be your mother, older
than my mother. Your mother's dead.
& last year both our fathers.
I've kept each secret you told me.

Poppies

By now I should understand brevity.

One day the tightly threaded pale pods unstitch to a chorus line
of orange crepe skirts.

Days later, fallen petals cupped with dew. The upright stalks
each with their purple eye, a royal-starred darkness.

Five years & there are days still, lifting a glass of ice-cold water to my lips,
I'm broken open.

Over the phone, the staccato breath of yet another friend now wandering
a hospital's fluorescent hallways.

My face pressed into the early morning bite of June cold.

Just When Everything Human Seemed Impossible, the Birds Arrived

I was out all day in need of signs.
Take caution
said the picked-over carcass of crow.

Clomp & step, nettle stung,
my loud, uncertain mind.
Even a pebble in my boot was portent.

Then, a mottled barred owl
sturdy on a limb,
head rotating, rotating

till it's gaze steadied on me.

Then

Once I was always waiting for that thing to happen, that very next thing, the sublime, unexpected, slipped under the wood door.

Evenings I'd stand on the front step of the house, too shy, even in solitude.

Who might arrive?
I understood just a fraction of my fear.
I promised myself I could go farther than my mother.

Go farther? She was already dead.

I reached my body into another century.
Even now, inside this day, I want to know a next certainty.
What would that be?

This morning, light gold-foiled on apartments across the Hudson.
The red cut of an ambulance. On the uptown subway a woman reading, her baby tied across her chest.

& still—having said all this—I think: No, I'm really still 25 & it's that lovely, sticky summer in New York when I'd walk through the Village wanting to stop every stranger & ask her to tell me one secret.

I never thought I was going to get old. Then I was.

& This World

wears a bulky coat. It's steel
blue shadow slips
then shows up at the curb
sprayed by dirty ice.

Two men push
a blunt back & forth between
their gloved fingers.
A woman sings into her device.

I'd like to lift the blue shadow
into my arms.
Stay close, the woman sings.
Never let me go.

Direction

I can't remember what I came to find.

Not the pen.   Not the porcelain coffee mug,
glasses.   The book.

Out of the room.   Then back in.
Then standing in the middle of the room.

Waiting.   & now the long day of doors opening, kids
dropping knapsacks, the trill of new video levels, snacks.

Mom, watch this! I hear someone shout in the room
where I'm alone looking for what

I can't remember I came to find.

Pleasure

All my life, my friend tells me, I was dragged around by lust.
She slices a piece of pecorino & lays it carefully over a section of green apple.

Honestly, she says, it yanked me down more alleys & into more palaces
than I can remember. Tethered, she laughs.

What a relief to be free of it, she says. Not that I longed to be free, not then.
Then I lived for it, but when it was gone, it was gone.

Suddenly, there is a good deal more to consider each day, she says.
Just washing plums & pears. You'll see.

The tilt of them drying on the cloth. Don't get me started on the cardinals.

Without Refuge

I wanted hazardous weather to bring our city to a muffled dawn,
salt trucks, the thick scrape of plows & every radio tuned for school closings.

When I went outside even the wind was dark & came to a stop at my side.
A pillar I could almost lean against.

The In-between

We slow at the park fence to watch a young father dribble & pass a
basketball to his girl & boy.

All that time on the playground, my friend says, but, if I'm honest,
I only remember a little this & that. Not even whole days with the kids.

The girl knocks the ball from the boy's hand & the father gives her the
thumbs-up, then tosses the ball back to the boy to try for another shot.

I was always rushing off to something important, my friend says. But
playing, she says, just fooling around with the kids, that's what I wish I
remembered better, the in-between.

Envy, 2020

Unlit alleys, fast rivers, all the far
distances I might have driven then beyond

to glittered clubs, crowded, pulsing hard.
How many more lips I wish I'd kissed,

touched the ribbed muscle of her thigh,
then turned a cheek to his silken wrist.

I envy now spring's tangle of limbs,
blossoms overlapping, each

offering promiscuously brief.

Ode after Menopause

I miss the blood.
The plush, thick insistence. Lunar declaration, my flag.
Then years living together, mysterious reconciling,
not that we were always a sister nation,
didn't bitch, get bitchy, blame everything
on a knot that bellied down, rumped me to my knees.
& those gym passes, Coach too embarrassed
to challenge how it stretched on for weeks.
Now I'm missing cash registers where I averted my eyes,
the rectangle box a public admission, & yes,
let's bless the shyness of teenage boys bagging,
handing back change & what happened
between us, a moment, electric—what was it?
—cringe, tease, apology, brag—
that we were actually bodies walking around
with the whole screwy, beautiful, damaged
human history of bodies. & bless too,
the anti-corporate, vinegar-cleansed sponges
& menstrual cup years I bannered to take back
body & night. & let this be praised:
how his cock looked crimson sheathed,
how his face came up smeary & I tasted iron on his tongue.
Destroyers, we were—sheets, mattress,
my own sticky fingers—our carnage, &

oh, that muscled relief of coming.
& then the just-after, cleaned-out days,
follicular, ovules burst, dropping luteal.
Call this batshit nostalgic, but here's to the crazy-making
late months, that haze of calculation & fret,
stalled in doorways practicing conversations I didn't want.
Once, on my knees in a summer field, I prayed.
Then the stain of forgiveness, like blessing.
Here, right now, an official thank you
to every public library, office, gas station, airplane,
restaurant, concert port-o-potty, state park bathroom
where, behind latched stalls, I angled in
smooth cardboard & also, too, to strangers,
ladies who helped when I was an empty purse,
not a scrounged coin to turn the metal dispensary
for this nest I shed month after month
after year after decade like it was nothing,
a tag-along, the occasional phew, other times the rebuke,
fertility failure, but never once did I acknowledge
did I really consider, what it gave the rest of me:
brain, skin, bones, tissues, memory, sleep, mood,
until it was gone. For months. Then back.
Back out of whack rollercoaster of a coda,
odd day, whole month wallops uncontainable,

dinners or meetings unfinished before torrent,
final rampage, this sorcery of woman
the ancients believed could stop lightning.
& then it stopped. Really. Forever. Period.

Only Paradise

Please know I would not strip back
      a single year from how we make love older

-bodied, your hip arthritic, rhythmic
      as I twist above or below, creaked-out knee,

wrecked, wracked & us, unrepaired, bone on
      bone, rocking ever closer toward arrival.

I want to make this rickety spectacle
      our chosen extinction, our lights out,

our no-good-night-to-go-easy
      final shebang. But enough of sweet pillow talk,

darling, get serious, get on your back, & let's blow out
      what's left of our voluptuous minds.

Do Over

All those years of worry when I might have chosen wonder.

O, that I could persuade that fevered stomp of girl to look up.

There, a woman at an open window, shaking out a yellow blanket.

Even Then

I was trying to be less.

Still raw wind delighted
the ferns.

Those afternoons, waiting
for water to boil.

Even then I cheated
at my game of solitaire.

& still didn't I feel victorious when I won?

Another Garden

We set cairns to find our way back.

      But we did not turn back. Ahead

the river branched. Swallows

      curved, dipped into dusk.

Midges hatched, sketched across

      inlets. We never turned

back. Before us, around us,

      a great unfathomable forest.

Then desert.

      When we were frightened

we tried to recall when we had stopped

      piling the great stone markers?

A gold dragonfly landed with net wings.

Another's iridescent blue wings. We stopped

worrying that fear would end. We did

not turn back. We had yet to imagine

something we could not imagine.

Though we would. & we had begun.

Notes

In my thinking about borders, migration, and expulsion, I've read and dipped into too many books to mention in these notes; however, here are a few. I have found particularly illuminating work on Genesis by Elaine Pagels and Avivah Gottlieb Zornberg. There are currently more than 272 million people who leave their homes for reasons of work, violence, climate, and political unrest. The United Nation World Migration Report is a good place to begin to consider global migration and displacement. And if a personal account helps de-abstract the numbers and situation, Luis Alberto Urrea's *The Devil's Highway* is a powerful account of 26 men trying to make their way from Mexico into the United States. And Francisco Cantú's memoir *The Line Becomes a River* is a chilling and complex insight into the border and border patrol in the Southwest.

"We Petition You, Sirs,": The start for this poem comes from and uses fragments of correspondence between 1947 and 1966 when my father and great uncle wrote letters to the Polish government and to the Foreign Claims Settlement Commission of the United States. In the first letters from 1947-8, my uncle, who escaped to Spain after internment in four different French concentration camps, tried to locate and learn the fate (exterminated) of his mother, sister, brother, and their offspring. Later letters are claims for property restitution and compensation for homes and property, though none was made. One letter from the Polish Ministry, August 3, 1965 states, "because of the destroyed records (from Warsaw), it is not possible to establish whether Abram Krancenblum was the owner." No acknowledgement of the deaths or restitution was ever made.

"Ordinary Sight": At age 24, the Dutch Portuguese philosopher Baruch Benedicto de Spinoza was excommunicated from his Amsterdam Jewish community. The official proclamation decreed, "That no one should communicate with him neither in writing nor accord him any favor nor stay with him under the same roof nor within four cubits in his vicinity;

nor shall he read any treatise composed or written by him." Lines from the herem—the text of excommunication—which was read from Amsterdam's Sephardic Synagogue's ark on July 27th 1656, are in italics in the first four stanza's of the poem whereas later italicized lines are taken from the writings of Spinoza.

"Brace" is dedicated to countless women and men who everyday manage extraordinary challenges of body and mind. On a more limited and, finally, temporary level, I was put into my first body brace for scoliosis at 13, which turned out to have been prescribed on the wrong side for my S curve. Between ages 14 and 22, I was corrected in a full body brace, the Milwaukee brace, a throat mold to pelvic corset attached with multiple vertical metal bars and various rib rotation pads. Protocol required 23 hours a day in the brace. Eventually I was weaned until the last year when allowed to only sleep in the body brace.

"Mount Lafayette Elegy, 1982" is dedicated to and in loving memory of Nancy Rockwell.

"Just When Everything Human Seemed Impossible, the Birds Arrived" is dedicated to Laurie Frankel, Kate Moses, Kate Carroll de Gutes, Elmaz Abinader, Shoba Rao, and the beautiful Hedgebrook cabin and staff who helped me find a path back from darkness.

"Pleasure" is dedicated to Martine Vermeulen.

Acknowledgments

Thank you to the editors who have published or commissioned some of these poems: *Poem-a-Day* at the Academy of American Poetry, *Big Other*, *Harvard Review*, Manchester Ripples of Hope Festival, *Salmagundi*, *Silent Auctions*, and *Speak*.

Thank you, thank you, Martha Rhodes, Ryan Murphy, Bridget Bell, and the Four Way Books team.

My forever gratitude to Bill Clegg and the folks at The Clegg Agency.

For insight, friendship, and encouragement in shaping my thinking about individual poems and the manuscript in its various incarnations, my abiding admiration and thanks to the wildly generous and brilliant Marie Howe, Donna Masini, Jessica Jacobs, Nickole Brown, Elizabeth Jacobson, Alan Michael Parker, Nick Flynn, Vievee Francis, Ricky Ian Gordon, Sophie Cabot Black, Michael Klein, Paisley Rekdal, Megan Fernandes, Jessica Redel, Honor Moore, Rachel Eliza Griffiths, Suzanne Gardinier, Fran Antell, Marty Moran, Martha Rhodes, and finally, my brothers, Ralph Angel and Richard McCann—man, I miss you.

Heart of my heart, Bruce Van Dusen, thank you for making me laugh before you've even poured my coffee and for the whole day that unspools.

More than love to Jonah Redel-Traub and Gabriel Redel-Traub who are still teaching me.

And thanks to the larger family: Zane, Ellen, Falcon, Sky Fox, Dara, Magnus, Ellis, Wynn, and Shea who have allowed me to begin teaching them the joy of tomatoes.

Thank you to the Rijksmuseum library, Hedgebrook, the Fine Arts Work Center, and the cabin at Lost Lake for providing necessary quiet and to Sarah Lawrence College for a course release's gift of time. I also thank my students, especially at Sarah Lawrence, for their endless curiosity and the great adventure of working together.

It's been a long time since I was a student, but I'm still guided every day by the wisdom, art, and generosity of my teachers and mentors: Richard Corum, Syd Lea, Grace Paley, Stanley Kunitz, Phil Levine, Joseph Brodsky, Varujan Boghosian, Dan Halpern, Derek Walcott, Adrienne Rich, Gerald Stern, Gordon Lish, and William Bronk.

Enduring gratitude and love to my parents, Natalie Soltanitzky and Irving Redel, and to my Nana, Devorah Soltanitzky, for the ways they carried the history, and to the elders I carry within.

Victoria Redel is the author of three previous collections of poetry and five books of fiction. A former recipient of Guggenheim and NEA fellowships, she teaches at Sarah Lawrence College.

Publication of this book was made possible by grants and donations. We are also grateful to those individuals who participated in our 2021 Build a Book Program. They are:
Anonymous (16), Maggie Anderson, Susan Kay Anderson, Kristina Andersson, Kate Angus, Kathy Aponick, Sarah Audsley, Jean Ball, Sally Ball, Clayre Benzadón, Greg Blaine, Laurel Blossom, Adam Bohannon, Betsy Bonner, Lee Briccetti, Joan Bright, Jane Martha Brox, Susan Buttenwieser, Anthony Cappo, Carla and Steven Carlson, Paul and Brandy Carlson, Renee Carlson, Alice Christian, Karen Rhodes Clarke, Mari Coates, Jane Cooper, Ellen Cosgrove, Peter Coyote, Robin Davidson, Kwame Dawes, Michael Anna de Armas, Brian Komei Dempster, Renko and Stuart Dempster, Matthew DeNichilo, Rosalynde Vas Dias, Kent Dixon, Patrick Donnelly, Lynn Emanuel, Blas Falconer, Elliot Figman, Jennifer Franklin, Helen Fremont and Donna Thagard, Gabriel Fried, John Gallaher, Reginald Gibbons, Jason Gifford, Jean and Jay Glassman, Dorothy Tapper Goldman, Sarah Gorham and Jeffrey Skinner, Lauri Grossman, Julia Guez, Sarah Gund, Naomi Guttman and Jonathan Mead, Kimiko Hahn, Mary Stewart Hammond, Beth Harrison, Jeffrey Harrison, Melanie S. Hatter, Tom Healy and Fred Hochberg, K.T. Herr, Karen Hildebrand, Joel Hinman, Deming Holleran, Lillian Howan, Thomas and Autumn Howard, Catherine Hoyser, Elizabeth Jackson, Jessica Jacobs and Nickole Brown, Christopher Johanson, Jen Just, Maeve Kinkead, Alexandra Knox, Lindsay and John Landes, Suzanne Langlois, Laura Lauth, Sydney Lea, David Lee and Jamila Trindle, Rodney Terich Leonard, Jen Levitt, Howard Levy, Owen Lewis, Matthew Lippman, Jennifer Litt, Karen Llagas, Sara London and Dean Albarelli, Clarissa Long, James Longenbach, Cynthia Lowen, Ralph and Mary Ann Lowen, Ricardo Maldonado, Myra Malkin, Jacquelyn Malone, Carrie Mar, Kathleen McCoy, Ellen McCulloch-Lovell, Lupe Mendez, David Miller, Josephine Miller, Nicki Moore, Guna Mundheim, Matthew Murphy and Maura Rockcastle, Michael and Nancy Murphy, Myra Natter, Jay Baron Nicorvo, Ashley Nissler, Kimberly Nunes, Rebecca and Daniel Okrent, Robert Oldshue and Nina Calabresi, Kathleen Ossip, Judith Pacht, Cathy McArthur Palermo, Marcia and Chris Pelletiere, Sam Perkins, Susan Peters and Morgan Driscoll, Patrick Phillips, Robert Pinsky, Megan Pinto, Connie Post, Kyle Potvin, Grace Prasad, Kevin Prufer, Alicia Jo Rabins, Anna Duke Reach,

Victoria Redel, Martha Rhodes, Paula Rhodes, Louise Riemer, Sarah Santner, Amy Schiffman, Peter and Jill Schireson, Roni and Richard Schotter, James and Nancy Shalek, Soraya Shalforoosh, Peggy Shinner, Anita Soos, Donna Spruijt-Metz, Ann F. Stanford, Arlene Stang, Page Hill Starzinger, Marina Stuart, Yerra Sugarman, Marjorie and Lew Tesser, Eleanor Thomas, Tom Thompson and Miranda Field, James Tjoa, Ellen Bryant Voigt, Connie Voisine, Moira Walsh, Ellen Dore Watson, Calvin Wei, John Wender, Eleanor Wilner, Mary Wolf, and Pamela and Kelly Yenser.

"'But doesn't every story begin with expulsion?' asks Victoria Redel in her lyrical revision of paradise from the distance of/ in time. 'We came from somewhere. Had a village, & then didn't,' she continues as pages turn in this powerful book of diaspora and exile. If Auden was right and Ireland 'hurt' Yeats into poetry, then certainly history 'hurts' Victoria Redel into most moving sonnets, list poems, invocations and spells of inter-generational memory. The reader will learn here of a grandfather who 'played flute in the orchestra of Turkish Sultan' and 'was nicknamed The Little Sultan by the Turkish Sultan himself.' Such scraps of memory, are they real, or are we making them up as consolation, watching our loved ones, one after another, disappear in time, Victoria Redel asks. What is most real to me is this poet's insistence on astonishment despite all the history—or maybe because of it: 'All those years of worry when I might have chosen wonder' she writes. Yes. Open this book on the poem called 'Pleasure' and you will be captivated, you will want to share these pages with your friends. I know I did. I wish you *Paradise*, readers. For that's where this beautiful book is taking you, as it re-envisions the meaning of the word."
—Ilya Kaminsky

"Redel leaps into the great mythical original maw of us—our shame, our guilt, our our our. The beginning of us, the end of us, the middle, which is still us. *Paradise* is a spiritual history of catastrophe and survival, described and reimagined by a traveler / witness / scribe who is one of us earthbound dreamers, an overtaker and escapee like us, whose 'new world' is already taken, already lived through. A glorious paradox of this work about migration, diaspora, goodbyes, regeneration, tremors and shifts, losses upon losses: the book acknowledges the bleak facts and trauma of empire, yet is simultaneously a rapturous read, a beautiful experience. To enter the atmosphere of Redel's poetic mind and perspective, winding and clear—to spend time in Redel's voice, sense of history, lang-scape—is heavenly because truth and beauty, at every turn of phrase and page, grows and spreads like mycelia, connecting all the journeys together at the buried, living roots. This book, breathing, is planted at the other end of Eden, and it gives me hope."
—Brenda Shaughnessy

Four Way Books / Poetry $16.95

Author photo: Sigrid Estrada
Book design: Maisonneke

ISBN 978-1-954245-13-6

US$16.95

51695>

9 781954 245136

Indirect Light

poems

Malachi Black